HOW TO AVOID THE FOUR -HEADED MONSTER:

Probate Court, Estate "Death" Tax, Financial Creditors & Predators, and Nursing Homes

PATRICK J. KELLEHER, ESQ.

Editorial Supervision - Erik Christensen and Steve White

Production Supervision: Erik Christensen

Book Design - Rachel Turner

First published in 2020 by Patrick J. Kelleher: ISBN: 978-1-7003-3630-9 (pbk.)

Library of Congress Cataloging-In-Publication Data

Kelleher. Patrick J.

How to Avoid the Four-Headed Monster: Probate Court, Estate Death Taxes, Financial Creditors & Predators and Nursing Homes

ISBN: 978-1-7003-3630-9

1. Probate Court   2. Estate Death Tax 3. Elder Care Law   4. Estate Planning

ISBN: 978-1-7003-3630-9

1st Edition February 2020

Printed in the United States of America

TABLE OF CONTENTS

FOREWORD

My partner Tom Foye and I launched the *South Shore Senior News* nearly four years ago, as we wanted to provide valuable resources to an ever-growing senior community.

Soon after we began publishing, a team member of Patrick Kelleher's Elder Law Care Center spotted our newspaper and saw that we shared not only a similar audience but the common goal of helping the senior population navigate their later years with expert information that would help them make informed decisions — especially on complex topics.

Patrick is a highly respected elder law attorney who has been teaching free educational estate planning and elder law workshops to seniors and volunteering in the community for over a decade.

Patrick is also a man on a mission, and that mission is to make sure elders and their loved ones are fully protected in the fourth quarter of their lives. And he does this by speaking from the heart, a passion fueled by what he saw up close and personal happen to his own family.

Patrick Kelleher has an amazing ability to connect with the elder population; I've seen it firsthand. He does it through personal anecdotes, humorous storytelling, and by giving off a vibe that says "I am not a salesperson. And, if I *am* selling anything, it's peace of mind." I've found him to be genuinely compassionate, and his enthusiasm is contagious; you can feel his energy and drive when he talks with seniors. He truly cares, and I admire this quality.

It really isn't surprising that Patrick chose to write this book. He has the expertise needed to help our aging population enjoy their later years without having to live in the dark shadow of knowing they could lose everything they've worked so hard for by making a bad decision, or no decision at all.

When it comes to elder law and the rights of our aging

population, Patrick Kelleher is their guardian at the gate. And the government, probate court, tax-man, nursing homes, and any other financial creditors or predators looking to take away what has been rightfully earned by his clients, best beware because Patrick's book will teach you how to protect what you have for the people you love the most.

Enjoy the book!

Patricia Abbate, Publisher,

South Shore Senior News

ACKNOWLEDGEMENTS

First, I give thanks to God for giving me the power and wisdom to write this book so that it may help you and your family protect what you have for the people you love the most. We are remembered in life for what we gave to the ones we loved the most and the contributions we made along the way. This book is for the common man and woman, as well as all walks of life, backgrounds and cultures. If you feel you worked hard for everything you have and you have a strong desire to *protect* it, *preserve* it and *pass* it down to your loved ones as a part of your legacy, then this book is for you! How would *you* like to be remembered?

I also thank my amazing parents, William and Ellen Kelleher, who sadly are no longer with me physically but are with me every day spiritually with the lessons they taught me, such as hard work, honesty, faith, education, gratitude and family. My parents being Irish immigrants had limited financial means when they arrived in America, but they grew rich with greatness throughout their lives with the selfless contributions they made to their seven sons.

I would also like to thank my colleagues and mentors, who are some of the best and brightest estate planning and elder law attorneys in the country, for the training and education they provided me. I am grateful to my literary agents, Erik Christensen and Steve White, for helping me share my message with you because you will now be armed with the sword and shield necessary to slay the "Four-Headed Monster" of Estate Planning & Elder Law that may try to stand in the way of your loved ones and your legacy.

Now, what are you going to do?

INTRODUCTION

"How did it get so late so soon?"

— *Dr. Seuss*

Who would have thought it would take the acclaimed author of such literary classics as *Green Eggs & Ham* to pretty much nail our mortality on the head?

The data states that 10,000 people turn 65 years of age every day in the U.S. and 70% of us 70 years of age will need some level of long-term care assistance someday. This can include nursing home care at the cost of about $15,000 or more per month in some states. The average stay in a nursing home is about three years. At $15,000 per month over a three-year period that is a whopping cost of $540,000!

The question you need to ask yourself is, if either you or your spouse become completely incapacitated, how will you pay for the $15,000 per month nursing home care?

Unlike fine wine we do not get better with age. Sadly,

I know all too well because it happened to both of my parents. My dad dying in a nursing home after he pledged he would never go into a nursing home and my mom making a courageous decision to go home on hospice after being diagnosed with a brain tumor. Both of these times were gut wrenching for me and my entire family.

Life isn't open-ended; we all come with an expiration date. The tricky part is we don't know the date on the calendar when Mother Teresa or Saint Peter will come calling. Let's face it, as much as you want to and as hard as you try, there often comes a point where you will no longer be able to care for yourself or an aging loved one. And in what is sure to be one of the most emotional times of your life, the last thing you want or need is the emotional stress associated with the steep cost of institutional care as it begins to siphon off your life savings. I personally went through this ordeal and it became rocket fuel for my passion, my purpose and my mission to help you and your loved ones avoid the "Four-Headed Monster of Estate Planning & Elder Law." Because of my experiences it became my calling to write this book so you can become an "informed consumer" and know how to protect what you have for the people you love the most.

I can recall it like it was just yesterday. My dad's health was rapidly declining and my mom was bravely trying to care for him at home. One day my dad took a bad fall at home and hit his head. The blood was terrifying to my mother. After my dad was rushed off by ambulance to the hospital the doctors determined it was no longer safe for him to return home because he was considered a fall risk. My father, a proud Irishman, was deeply saddened, but realized that it was safer for him and my mother for him to move to a rehabilitation facility and then, ultimately, a nursing home.

The downward spiral of aging and the economic and emotional slippery slope of long-term care had begun.

While my family worried about dad's declining health, I began to worry over how my parents would pay for the long-term healthcare, knowing full well some nursing facilities costs upwards of $15,000 per month. It was a horrible feeling. Would my parents lose the family home they worked their entire lives to pay for? I made the decision that this was a scenario that was *not* going to play out, not on my watch. I made the decision to put all my time and effort into furthering my studies and education in the field of elder law because I wanted to make sure that you and your family would become an informed consumer and have an opportunity to "take action" and put an estate and elder law plan in place before the shoe dropped. No more procrastination, no more uncertainty of what to do and how to do it.

Continue to read because within the pages of this book you will learn life changing steps and a *true-and-tried* proven "three-step" estate planning process that will help you protect your assets for those you love the most. This book will give you clear and decisive action steps so that you can build your very own family Trust or "Treasure Chest" so when the inevitable strikes you are protected and well prepared. *"The time to repair a leaking roof is when the sun is shining."* — *John F. Kennedy*

Plus, we'll delve deeply and thoroughly into the dreaded "Four-Headed Monster" of Estate Planning & Elder Law, which is — Probate Court, Estate "Death" Taxes, Financial Creditors & Predators, and Nursing Homes—by teaching you "The Three-Step Treasure Chest Process" you will need to slay this beast before it takes a massive bite out of your family assets and relationships forever.

Read on because you will learn and save a lot!

I hope you enjoy the book!

Patrick

WHY YOU NEED TO CREATE YOUR ESTATE PLAN *NOW!*

When it comes to creating wills, trusts and estate plans, as members of the Baby Boomer Generation we outpace our younger counterparts. Still, according to recent data 19% of those over the age of 72 and 42% of those between the ages of 53 and 71, lack any type of estate plan. And if you fall within those two categories you are putting your family and loved ones at significant risk.

Although managing these details can seem daunting and depressing at first, the task becomes far less unpleasant with proper understanding of the planning process. The process of creating an estate plan and protecting your family can also be personally gratifying and calming because it will give you immense peace of mind knowing that you took action to protect your loved ones. Estate planning is critically important for seniors and for their family members, who need to be prepared in the event of a loved one's illness or passing, because without a written plan the consequences can be extremely costly for your family members. Not just financially costly, but emotionally and mentally costly for your entire family.

They say 6 out of 10 people in the U.S. don't even have a Will. I often say to my clients, a Will is a good starting point, but from my experience a Will is woefully insufficient to properly protect your assets. In fact, a Will is your "Admission Ticket" to probate court.

How do you want to be remembered? When you don't put a plan in place, who stands to benefit?

If you or an aging loved one have been putting off estate planning, take action now while you are "alive and well" because if you wait until you are "alive and not so well" your family will be left behind to suffer the consequences.

Understanding the meaning of "estate"

In addition to the fear factor of planning for illness and death, many seniors dismiss its importance because they don't understand what "estate" means, or they believe it applies only to those with significant wealth. In reality, an estate includes everything you own, from your home(s), bank accounts, retirement accounts and life insurance to your automobiles, personal property and other assets.

Also, planning for your eventual disability is of the utmost importance because disability planning is one of the most overlooked areas in estate planning and often the first shoe to drop for all of us. Sadly, and inevitably, most of us will become incapacitated at one time or another, and when you do not have proper disability planning in place the "Disability Probate" process can be very expensive and costly for your family in terms of loss of money, time and unnecessary stress. I call this the "economic and emotional stresses and messes" of probate court.

The estate plan's role in self-advocacy

Estate plans help seniors establish important guidelines that allow them to advocate for themselves. This is essential for seniors who wish to retain their independence and protect their assets. In addition to creating Wills, Trusts and other important legal documents, an estate plan allows seniors to have a say in the quality of their long-term care — whether at home or in an assisted living facility — and to qualify for government benefits, such as Medicaid to help pay for that care. It also helps them to protect their life savings and outline their wishes should they become incapacitated or die unexpectedly. When you don't plan, you are inviting strangers from the probate court to manage your financial affairs and make your medical decisions when you become incapacitated. Even if you are married your spouse does not have legal authority to do this unless you have properly appointed them in the proper legal documents prior to your disability.

Establishing Trusts or Your "Treasure Chest"

Estate planning also includes provisions for developing Trusts. Trusts allow seniors to set aside money for specific people to avoid the long, drawn out, expensive and stressful process of probate court. Once your Trust, or what I like to call your "Treasure Chest," is properly funded with your assets it will allow your loved ones to receive their inheritances much quicker and with far less cost. And if the Trust is drafted properly, they can also receive asset protection from their potential financial creditors and predators (should your in-laws turn into outlaws) during times of turmoil; such as, lawsuits, automobile accidents or divorces (when your in-laws turn into outlaws).

While many Trusts are revocable, meaning the senior can change or terminate the Trust at any time, Irrevocable Trusts are often used to protect assets of a senior from the costs of the $15,000 per month price-tag often associated with the nursing home. With the staggering costs of long-term care and the average stay in the nursing home of about three years, it can cost you a whopping $540,000 to reside in a nursing home for those three years.

Also, keep in mind there is a "Five Year Look-Back" period when protecting your home from the nursing home. If your goal for your family is to protect and preserve the family home from the nursing home, you need to take action now because the clock does not start running until the day your home is funded or transferred into your Irrevocable Medicaid Asset Protection Trust (MAPT).

So how does the "Five Year Look-Back" period work? Let's use for an example a woman I will call Kathy. Kathy's house has a lot of equity in it. We transfer that house equity into her "Treasure Chest" (we'll talk more about the "Treasure Chest" in Chapter 5) and record the deed at her local registry of deeds. This triggers the five-year clock to begin running on the Medicaid Trust.

So now, as the clock begins to run, it's your job to

stay healthy. You eat lots of fruits and vegetables, take up active hobbies such as gardening, maybe even pull out that old "Sweatin' to the Oldies" videocassette. Maybe take the dog for a walk more than once a day. You need to try and stay healthy for the next five years. The old look-back period used to be three years. But now you have to stay healthy for five years, not incapacitated, not filing the Medicaid application because your assets will not be protected until the 5th anniversary of getting your property into your Trust or Treasure Chest.

Say we did all this for Kathy back in September 2017. Now we look into the future, when it's September 2022. The shoe drops. Kathy's boyfriend calls on a Monday morning — it's always a Monday morning — and he says Kathy's alive but not doing so well. She became disabled on Friday, to the point that she's completely incapacitated. She might have to go into a nursing home and pay privately. He then asks me if her house is protected. I open the file and say, yes, because Kathy took action in September 2017. She ate her fruits and vegetables, walked Fido numerous times a day, and sweated her buns off to "Sweatin' to the Oldies." Kathy stayed healthy for five years and a day. She legally beat the five year look-back period for MassHealth Medicaid planning. Now we fill out a MassHealth Medicaid application for Kathy. And when the question pops up, "Have you transferred any assets within the past five years?" you can truthfully answer that you have *not* transferred any assets in the past five years because it has been greater than five years. The goal is to get Kathy approved for MassHealth Medicaid benefits so they will pay for her nursing home care. The asset that Kathy transferred into her irrevocable Medicaid Asset Protection Trust (MAPT) a little over five years ago, her home, is protected for her family and for her loved ones. I call this the 3 Ps. Kathy *protected, preserved* and *passed* her home down to her loved ones creating a family legacy.

If you or your loved one have been avoiding this important planning responsibility, now is the time to begin, especially if you are 65 years of age or older. Being proactive increases your success in protecting what you have for the people you love the most. And the best time to plan is when you are "alive and well" compared to being "alive and not so well," like when you are incapacitated. Do not wait until life's two minute warning to think you can throw a "Hail Mary pass" and be successful in protecting your family. If you do, who knows who may pick off your pass? The Probate Court, the Tax-man, Financial Creditors & Predators, and/or the Nursing Home.

THE THREE W'S OF ESTATE PLANNING

A great scholar and visionary, Benjamin Franklin once observed, "By failing to plan, you are planning to fail." And although he probably wasn't thinking about estate planning when he uttered those words back in the late-1700s, some 300 years later they still ring true.

When it comes to estate planning, I always suggest to my clients that they adhere to the three W's—What, Who and Why. This should be your roadmap when it comes time to decide if and when the time is right to put things in motion.

The WHAT... is all about what you have that you are the most concerned about losing. Maybe it's your house, your retirement fund, your bank account, or your investments. For most people over the age of 65 that distinction falls to their home, both for monetary reasons (you could have upwards of $400,000-$500,000 or more in equity wrapped up in it) and for sentimental reasons (it's where you raised your family). Chances are very good that you have become emotionally attached to your home and to suddenly lose it through the lack of or poor estate planning, and no longer have it available to pass on to your children, would be a tragedy.

The WHO… is usually to protect the people you love most, whether it be your spouse, your children, your grandchildren, or all of the above. It's hardwired in your parental instinct to protect your young ones (one of the major reasons we steer clear of mother bears).

Your WHO… is probably staring at you right now while you're sitting at home reading this book. Take a look around your house. Maybe the "Who" is sitting on a mantel piece over your fireplace, or hanging on the living room wall, or resting prominently on your nightstand so it's the first thing you see when you wake up in the morning. That picture of your family is the "Who," nicely summed up in an 8x10 or 24x36 inch picture frame, for the entire world to see or like lots of my clients the digital family photos on your smart phone and on Facebook.

The WHY...is the reason you are driven and motivated to create your estate plan, Will, Trust and Treasure Chest. Because nobody makes you do estate planning. Your WHY could be because you do not want the State or government getting what you worked so hard for. Your Why could be you want to make things easy for your spouse and children when you're gone and want to make sure your family still gets along and doesn't fight and spend outrageous amounts of money in the drawn out probate court process (avoid the stresses and messes of probate court). Your WHY can be that you feel you already paid enough taxes in your lifetime and you do not want the tax-man becoming an involuntary beneficiary of your estate for the estate "death" tax if you have a taxable estate. (Massachusetts current estate tax amount is 1 Million dollars). Your WHY could be like lots of our clients who feel they worked very hard for their family assets and want to give their three beautiful children Moe, Larry and Curly a "protected" gift and not an unprotected gift like a Will and most standard trust plans give. Or your WHY could be you have heard or seen family, friends or neighbors lose the family home to the nursing home after a loved one became incapacitated.

So when you think about it, the *three W's — What, Who* and *Why*—all have one thing in common; protecting your family and loved ones. That's what estate planning is all about, protecting what you have for those you love because nobody makes you do it. The government does not require you to do it. I call it taking that immense "personal responsibility" to protect what you have for the people you love the most. It all boils down to an act of love. Don't let anyone take it away from you because when you don't plan properly (A Will doesn't cut it) who stands to benefit? Take action NOW!

YOUR DREAM SNAPSHOT

When folks come to my educational estate planning and elder law workshops, they all pretty much give the same answer when I ask them, "Why are you here?" They will say I need a Will, or I need a Trust. And then I'll say, "That's fine, but before we make a determination on whether you need a Will or a Trust, let's do a little exploration. Let's find out about your goals, your concerns, your dreams, and your vision for your family. Let's talk about your Dream Snapshot."

Before I go into detail on what exactly a "Dream Snapshot" is, let's first agree that when it comes to estate planning, it is not a one-size-fits-all scenario. Everyone approaches estate planning with different goals, different concerns, different family dynamics, different things that keep you up at night. You have to create an estate plan

31

around your unique family situation. And this is where your Dream Snapshot comes into focus, so to speak.

In order to define your Dream Snapshot, let's do a little exercise. Picture yourself up on your cloud many years from now. Imagine it's a beautiful day, temperature in the mid-70s, blue skies, gentle breeze, Red Sox are playing out at Fenway Park, and you're looking down on the front side of the cloud at your family, and they all seem very happy. They're all getting along, they're talking, they're communicating, they look happy.

Conversely, let's turn our attention to the backside of the cloud. Hmm, not so good. The sky is dark, you hear thunder, see lightning flashes, and, uh-oh, here comes the heavy rain. You're looking down at your family and they don't look happy. They're not getting along. They seem to be arguing, fighting about money. Now you see probate litigation attorneys showing up in their pinstripe suits, carrying leather brief cases because your family can no longer communicate civilly with each other. This is *not* the snapshot you want to see. This from my experience is an estate plan that did not work.

Many times that Dream Snapshot we *want* to avoid comes to fruition when mom passes away. This is because in most cases the mom is the matriarch of the family, the glue that holds everything together. So when mom passes away that glue becomes undone, and the result is the kids are unsettled. And if the estate plan wasn't done properly before mom's passing, then it's off to the probate court for about a year and a half, maybe even two years or longer. Then it's usually one child assigned to be in charge (executor now called personal representative or trustee) to work with the probate or estate attorney. It's a lot of work to put on the shoulders of a child, to do that job by themselves. However, from my experience when your estate plan has clear instructions and the personal representative or trustee follows those instructions, you will achieve your Dream Snapshot or the front side of the cloud. The personal representative or trustee of the estate has what the law calls a "fiduciary duty of loyalty" to act in the best interest of the estate and the beneficiaries of the estate. Part of their responsibility is to follow the written instructions in their loved ones Will and Trust and communicate well with all of the beneficiaries of the estate, not a chosen few. When your personal representative or trustee fails to meet their fiduciary obligations or acts carelessly or allows their ego or ulterior motives to influence them this can cloud their judgment and can have devastating consequences for your Dream Snapshot and your family's future harmony. When this happens, all of a sudden there's this big secret going on. It's like Sgt. Schultz in *Hogan's Heroes,* — "I see nothing! I hear nothing! I know nothing!" It becomes a very unpleasant experience for everyone and really has a detrimental effect on family relationships. I've seen it happen quite often. Don't let it happen to your family.

Make sure you're on the front side of the cloud by taking action to put a proper estate plan in place while you're alive and well and by picking a suitable personal representative or trustee to manage your Treasure Chest after you are gone. Do not let your personal representative or trustee "helper" fly your cozy Dream Snapshot cloud into the side of a mountain. This can be avoided by your picking a suitable family member to be your future disability and death trustee or helper. I often say to my clients you are the expert on the family and we are the expert on estate planning and elder law. You teach us about the family and we teach you about the law. The deal is we work together to create a plan that will meet your Dream Snapshot!

The good news is our "Three-Step Treasure Chest Process" comes with a "Trustee Training" program and educational workshops that will teach our trustee helpers how to be successful with your Dream Snapshot cloud.

THE IMPORTANCE OF HOLDING A FAMILY CAREGIVING MEETING

A family caregiving meeting is an essential tool when dealing with the care of an aging loved one. These meetings are beneficial for helping to keep all family members abreast of decisions that need to be made, changes in diagnosis or prognosis, and to help ensure that all family members feel that they have a voice. Family meetings can also help to keep caregiving responsibilities from falling solely on the shoulders of one family member. In addition, family caregiving meetings can foster cooperation among family members and lessen the stress associated with caring for an aging loved one. Good communication and transparency among immediate family members is paramount to fostering healthy relations and harmony.

Who should attend a family caregiving meeting?

First and foremost, it is important to include the aging loved one in the meeting whenever possible. This helps the aging loved one to feel that they are being heard and that their opinions and thoughts are being considered. If a spouse is living, the spouse should be included, as well as any children and possibly siblings of the aging person. Some families may choose to include other family members, but this really varies from one family to another. From my experience immediate family members work best in the "Family Care Meeting" which would exclude in-laws.

Anyone else involved in medical care for the person should attend a separate "Medical Care Meeting" that would include paid caregivers, geriatric case managers, doctors and other medical professionals. Depending on family dynamics, a facilitator can be helpful in running the meeting.

When should a family have a caregiving meeting?

It is important to note that family caregiving meetings are not a one and done event. They must occur on a regular basis. The first family meeting should occur before an aging loved one actually needs care. This can give the person who may eventually need care more say in their future care. However, most families find that the initial meeting needs to occur when an aging loved one begins to show signs of needing care, or when a diagnosis is given that determines care will soon be needed. In addition, meetings should be scheduled regularly to discuss changes in diagnosis, prognosis, or general needs of the loved one or the caregivers.

How can a family hold a successful caregiving meeting?

The key to having a successful caregiving meeting is cooperation. This doesn't mean that family members will agree on everything, but it is important that all family members are respectfully heard and considered.

Families must be willing to compromise and seek the best plan for their aging loved one. Additionally, a smoothly run meeting should have an agenda and families should try to stay focused on the items included on the agenda. When holding a meeting, always put things in writing and be sure that all those involved get a copy of the important information and everyone's responsibilities.

What challenges do families face in caregiving meetings?

One of the biggest challenges is the family's history. All families have their own dynamics that can cause problems in a caregiving meeting. There may be members of the family who are at odds with one another, thereby creating an obstacle to having a successful caregiving meeting. The role that each family member plays can be a challenge. Some members may be aggressive, overbearing and demand control, while others are peacemakers and do not feel free to share their thoughts. Another challenge is that some family members may be in denial of the severity of an aging loved one's needs, which could make it difficult to get a consensus for care.

Family caregiving meetings are beneficial and necessary when an aging loved one can no longer care for themselves. These meetings can help to divide the responsibilities of caregiving and reduce stress placed on the family members. It is important that families remember that the meetings are for the care of their loved one and cooperate with one another to help the process run smoothly and successfully. Again, clear communication, transparency, regular updates, respect and allowing each immediate family member's (children of parent) voice to be heard is critical to ensure on-going family harmony.

THE THREE-STEP TREASURE CHEST PROCESS™

The dictionary defines a process as "a series of actions or steps taken in order to achieve a particular end." And when it comes to designing and creating your estate plan, that "end" is simply to protect your assets from the probate court, the tax-man, ("the State"), financial creditors and predators and the nursing home, also known as, the "Four-Headed Monster" of Estate Planning & Elder Law. Each is like a monster trying to eat away everything you worked your entire life for. Bottom-line: you should not be punished for getting old.

This process involves three separate courses of action, which is why I refer to it as a "Three-Step Treasure Chest Process"™. My firm has helped hundreds of clients and their families with our Three Step Process. Colleagues of mine across the country that use a Three Step Process also have helped their clients avoid the Four Headed Monster. The Three Step Process has collectively helped thousands of families save hundreds of thousands of dollars and helped the clients obtain their Dream Snapshot putting them on the front side of the cloud happily smiling down on their loved ones.

It is the Three Step Process that works because the old school way of estate planning has been proven not to work for families. The old school way is lame and outdated because it is typically a one-time event or transaction of people buying "a stack of documents" whether those documents are a Trust or a Will that do not work. They do not work because the legacy studies show that on average a period of 18.2 years goes by before someone ever looks at that stack of documents again. It usually occurs with the passing of the client when the family calls the lawyer to report their loved ones death. The estate plan does not work because we have found that the 3 L's have crept into that plan over the 18.2 years. The 3 L's are, Changes in *Law*, Changes in *Life* and Changes in *Learning* in the industry. How much control do we have over changes in law? How often does congress change the tax code? How many of you have the same health, finances and relationships as you did five years ago? How many changes in learning have been made in the Trust and estate industry? Now, after the 3 L's what is wrong with your estate plan? It's *OUTDATED!* From my experience an outdated estate plan will ***not*** work to meet your goals or vision.

What works best from our experience of helping thousands of families is the Three-Step Process. That is the magic formula to achieving the front side of the cloud for you and your family. You need to follow this process in order to protect what you have worked hard for, especially if you want to do the 3 P's, which is *Protect*, *Preserve* and *Pass* down what you have to your loved ones as a family legacy.

Step One

Step One of our Three-Step Treasure Chest Process (3STCP)™ is to first learn from our clients what is most important to them. We do the requisite counseling and learn about the clients' "Dream Snapshot" and then we design their plan in a "Trust Design" meeting by drawing the clients' Trust, Will and ever so important disability documents (The Big 6) on the white board. We ask the clients who they would like to help them during the time of their disability (disability trustee) and at the time of their death (death trustee). I refer to the "Trust Design" meeting as the heart and soul of the estate planning process because this is where your plan is constructed, engineered and built with your input and your estate planning and elder law attorney guiding you along the way like your personal architect and custom builder. After your Dream Snapshot is created in the "Trust Design" our clients return to our office in about a week or two later to sign their Trust centered estate plan. Hooray, their Trust is designed and signed and step one is completed. However, the estate plan is not a magic book because Steps 2 and 3 need to be completed for the clients plan to truly work.

Step Two (Read Caution on Trust Funding Qualified Retirement Accounts, 401ks, IRAs etc.)

If we did not complete Step 2 the clients' Trust plan is nothing more than a big fancy expensive paper weight. It will not work because "Asset Titling" is one of the most important things in estate planning. This step is so critical to the success of your estate plan it bears repeating again. "Asset Titling" is one of the most important things in estate planning because that is where all the magic happens. That is how you obtain all the protections from the Four-Headed Monster. How your assets are titled will determine whether they go off to the probate court when you become disabled and die. How your assets are titled will determine your tax obligation to the tax man for estate "death" tax. How your assets are titled will determine whether your spouse and children will have asset protection from financial creditors and predators in times of turmoil. How your assets are titled will determine whether Medicaid or the nursing home will place a lien on your family home and assets if you or your spouse became completely incapacitated.

You need a metaphorical treasure chest to hold your valuables in. When I teach my educational Estate Planning & Elder Law workshops, I illustrate this point by holding up an actual old-school looking treasure chest. But the point remains the same; you typically should "fund, title or transfer" your assets into your Trust or Treasure Chest to protect what you have for the people you love the most). **(with the exception of your qualified retirement accounts; 401K, IRAs etc.)** This process is called "Trust

Funding" and it is one of the most overlooked areas in estate planning yet ironically it is a critical step to ensure the success of your estate plan. **Caution: You never should fund, transfer, title or change ownership of your qualified retirement accounts, 401ks or IRAs, etc. directly into your trust because this would cause a taxable event for you and you could end up with a big tax bill. Do not do trust funding yourself. We strongly advise that you work with a qualified attorney who is familiar with trust funding in your jurisdiction because the laws and rules can be different and the consequences for you could be great.** My firm helps our clients with this step because we have a formal trust funding process. My trust funding coordinator works with our clients by drafting all of the trust funding instruction letters and verification letters to our clients' banks, financial institutions, life insurance companies, deeds for properties, and other assets.

We instruct the holder of your assets to retitle your

asset from your name as an "individual" to your name as "trustee" of the asset. For example, Bill and Mary hold the title to their home and bank accounts in their names individually. We typically re-title the asset from Bill and Mary, Individually to Bill and Mary, as trustees of Bill and Mary's Trust. We refer to this as "trust funding" or "asset titling," and this is one of the most important areas of estate planning. How your assets are held will be a determining factor as to whether those assets end up in probate court in a time of disability or death leaving your family to endure the economic and emotional headaches of probate court. If you have a taxable estate and your estate planning or elder law attorney drafted the proper estate tax planning language in your Trust you want to make sure your assets are funded to your Trust during your lifetime.

If you desire an enhanced level of asset protection for your surviving spouse and children, then it is very important to have your assets funded to your Trust during your lifetime to protect them from financial creditors and predators. My clients feel they worked hard for their money and they want to pass it along to their loved ones with some level of asset protection. My clients want to leave more than an inheritance "outright in the palms of hands" to their beneficiaries because they realize this common way of leaving assets offers zero protections. I call that leaving your loved ones an *unprotected* gift because during times of turmoil how much of that inheritance are you putting at risk? That's correct, all of it, 100% is at risk to your loved ones lawsuits, bankruptcies, automobile accidents, and at least 50% at risk *when* your in-laws turn into outlaws during a divorce.

The Casserole Brigade and Betty the Barmaid

My client's dad let's say "Bob" has decided to sell his house and move to Florida after the death of a spouse. Since he's a very popular guy among all the widowers on his cul-de-sac, he finally hooks up with "Betty the Bar Maid" who is a member of the Casserole Brigade. That is what my Florida colleagues jokingly call the single ladies in Florida looking for new husbands because women often outlive and outnumber men in the cozy gated communities. Back to the story. The Casserole Brigade was courting Bob by welcoming him to the neighborhood with their best cooked dishes, such as, meatloaf, lobster mac 'n cheese, lasagna, tuna casserole etc. Bob picks the best cook, Betty, and they get married. Bob, being a standup guy, decides to change his will naming Betty the primary beneficiary and now his son has been bumped to a secondary role or as the contingent back-up beneficiary. Then one day Bob passes away and everything he owned went to his new bride, Betty. A few years later Betty dies. Bob's son calls his father's Florida attorney who does not return his phone calls. Bob's son hired me to investigate the matter because he understood that he was his dad's back-up beneficiary and next in line to receive his inheritance. I contact the Florida attorney asking to get information on his father's three houses so he can start making some plans. Here's the bad news: When Bob died, Betty went to her attorney and had her own Will created. Who do you think Betty named as her beneficiaries? That's right...Betty named her own children and left everything to **her family**... with nothing left for Bob's son. A sad story, but a true story.

Bob likely never fathomed in a million years that this would happen or that this could happen. This situation is more common than one would think because a Will does not provide any asset protection and is typically woefully insufficient to protect your loved ones. What was needed in this situation was some lock-down language in a Trust centered estate plan that put in place "family bloodline" protections that stated after Bob died his bride Betty could not remove his son as the back-up beneficiary. A very expensive and hurtful lesson for Bob's son.

Step Three

This is perhaps the most important step because although the day you sign your estate plan is important, what truly is *the most* important day you need it to work? Yes, that is correct, the day you check out or the day Mother Teresa comes calling. Legacy studies show that the average time of 18.2 years goes by from the time a person signs their estate plan. During those 18.2 years the 3 L's creep into that estate plan and outdate it. The 3 L's are Changes in LAW, Changes in LIFE (with your health, finances and relationships) and Changes in LEARNING in the estate and elder law industry. And it can happen in so many directions it will make your head spin, *if* you don't pay attention. It's critical that you monitor all your Trust or Treasure Chest and do not let it collect dust because if you do, your estate plan likely will not work to meet your vision. You may get the "backside" of the cloud or Dream Snapshot and not the desired front side of the cloud. And when I work with clients I make sure we do an annual review. But it's a two-way street. I may know about a change in the law, but chances are I am not going to know that you had a new grandchild or your son or daughter filed for bankruptcy or was going through a divorce, or you or someone serving an important role in your estate plan had a health change. Communication is key and I call it a two-way street. If there has been a change in law then your attorney should be contacting you to update your trust, if there has been a change in your life you should be contacting your attorney to keep your plan updated. These steps are necessary to beat the Four-Headed Monster!

One of the biggest problems or flaws in the estate planning industry is that estate planning (creating your Will or Trust) has always been and still is treated like an event or a transaction. A "one and done"; I got my Will, I can now check off the box on my to-do list and throw the Will in my lockbox and never ever have to look at it again. Who would, it's a legal document related to your death. But that is where the problem is because when you treat your estate plan like a transaction or event it will collect dust and the 3 L's will creep into it and it will become outdated. From my experience an outdated estate plan does not work.

I will tell you from my experience that in that 18.2 years you are likely to see five to six LAW changes, five to six LIFE changes, and five to six changes in LEARNING in the estate and elder law industry. That's up to 18 changes that can wreak havoc with a Will or Trust, *simply because no one was monitoring it.*

The Process is What Works

Rather than treating your estate plan like an event

or transaction that is doomed for failure, treat it like a process. We have learned that a process is the key to the success of our clients' estate plans. I call our process the "Three Step Treasure Chest Process" or step 3 of our process is what ensures that your Trust or treasure chest will continue to work as you journey through the path of life. We work with our clients and conduct annual reviews for members of our Client Care Program (CCP) or "Legacy Shield"™ program. The client pays a reasonable flat price annually and we keep their plan updated and working so when the shoe drops, the Four-Headed Monster will be defeated and your family will be safe!

The point is you have to believe that everything you have stored away in your Treasure Chest is alive; it's a living and breathing Treasure Chest that holds your most valuable and lifelong accumulated assets. What you and your spouse worked very hard for. You need to keep a close eye on your Treasure Chest and not ignore it because if you turn your back on it and fail to keep it updated as you journey through the path of life, who will be waiting to take a big juicy bite out of it? And it's the major reason you need a qualified estate planning or elder law attorney to keep track on what is changing and how it affects what's inside the Chest. I recommend working with an attorney who has a process and who will not charge you by the hour every time you call or email the law office with a question because that traditional way of planning does not work well for the client.

You need to protect your Treasure Chest from the 3 L's, which are changes in LAW (i.e. Medicaid regulations), changes in LIFE (i.e. death of a spouse), and changes in LEARNING (i.e. how laws and language are now determined). Even the best plans will become outdated at one time or another.

Remember, estate planning is a process, not a transaction.

And if you don't pay attention to the process, the assets you are holding — Wills, Trusts, etc. — are simply just a one-way ticket to probate court. And I can tell you from experience, it will be a very expensive trip.

Everything we have talked about in the last five chapters is geared towards making sure you know how to safely accumulate and protect all your valuable assets before the day comes when words like "probate," "nursing homes," "estate taxes," and "financial predators" start creeping into the twilight of your life. And when that day does come, and it will, you will want to make sure you partner with someone who will go to battle with you to slay the *"Four-Headed Monster."*

THE FOUR-HEADED MONSTER™

THE FOUR-HEADED MONSTER™: *PROBATE COURT - TWO TYPES; DEATH PROBATE & DISABILITY PROBATE*

DEATH PROBATE

I hear it all the time from clients; "I'm all set, right, I *have* a Will?" They say it like it's Willy Wonka's Golden Ticket, or a get-out-of-jail-free card. But in reality your Will is your "admission ticket" to probate court. And that is a very expensive trip you do not want to take. I call this the economic and emotional headaches of probate court.

Probate court is a very slow, court-driven process that can easily last 12-18 months, and often times longer. A woman attending one of my educational elder law workshops spoke up recently and said, "Patrick, I just finished the probate process and it took us eight years to complete it and nobody in the family talks to each other anymore." The gentlemen behind her spoke up and said, "Patrick, I just started the probate process for my mother who died and I'm hemorrhaging (financially) and I'm here because I want to put a Trust plan in place so my children do not have to go through what I'm going through."

Probate Court is a legal minefield with complex court rules that often require you to hire a probate court attorney to navigate all of the steps and paperwork involved. It is like the Roman Coliseum where the process is open to the public, puts creditors like Medicaid and MassHealth on notice for them to lien your estate and invites disgruntled family members to dispute the estate. Your personal representative (executor) pays the probate attorney by the hour with the meter running by the minute, and your personal representative can be held personally liable to the estate and its beneficiaries if they do not do their job correctly. The whole process is lengthy, costs a lot and creates undue and unnecessary stress on the entire family when they are often mourning and grieving the loss of a loved one. Unfortunately, this often leads to a lot of family in-fighting. The legal fees can cost up to a whopping 5% of your gross estate because Massachusetts does not have a statutory cap on legal fees. That's correct; the meter just keeps on running as long as the probate process is being worked on. To put the numbers in perspective, from my experience, if you have a one million dollar estate, it could cost you as much as $50,000 in legal fees because probate attorneys typically charge by the hour. Ouch! You have to ask yourself, whose pocket is that money coming out of? That's correct, your beneficiaries, your loved ones. The good news is there is a much better way.

DISABILITY PROBATE

Disability probate is one of the most overlooked areas in estate planning. Unlike fine wine we do not get better with age. From a statistical, actuarial standpoint most people will become disabled or incapacitated before they pass away. We will discuss the meat and potatoes of disability planning that everyone should have. I call them the "Big 6" disability planning tools you need in your tool-box or part of your Treasure Chest Plan.

Here's a little history. Between 2009 and 2012 Massachusetts adopted what they call the Massachusetts Uniform Probate Code (MUPC). These are the laws that govern and oversee Wills, probate and estates. As a result, the power of attorney law became outdated, meaning any power of attorneys older than July 1, 2009 may not work because the old law, Massachusetts General Law Chapter 201B, was repealed and taken off the law books. We update our clients Financial Durable power of attorney every year or every other year because if you become incapacitated and your Power of Attorney document doesn't work your loved ones will be off to the Probate Court for an expensive trip asking the good judge to appoint them as your conservator to make your financial decisions. The risk of using an older outdated power of attorney is far too great because in the real world it comes down to an issue of persuasion and if the decision maker, be it the banker or financial institution, doesn't like your power of attorney they may not accept it.

For instance, if you have power of attorney and you're completely disabled and your loved one, child or spouse goes into the bank and the branch manager isn't aware of the situation and they want to withdraw $10,000 from mom's account, it's been our experience that if the power of attorney is two or three years old, they typically don't accept it. Then what do you do? You need to go to the probate court and petition the judge for a conservatorship, while you pay your probate attorney by the hour throughout the entire process.

Another example: A client's wife is suffering in a local institution with severe dementia. She never signed a power of attorney. Despite nearly 50 years of marriage, the poor husband had zero legal authority to help his wife. So now the husband needs to manage her financial affairs so he can move her from the hospital to a nursing home facility. And he can't do that unless he has financial and medical authority to do so. He needs a legal Conservatorship to manage her financial affairs and a legal Guardianship to manage her healthcare affairs. The entire process took about nine months of legal work and the Court appointed a Guardian Ad Litem (GAL) for his wife which delayed the process. End result, our client incurred legal fees of about $10,000 before both orders were signed off by the judge. Our client was very stressed by the whole ordeal of seeing his lifelong partner decline in health before his eyes, as well as, feeling helpless and hopeless having no authority or powers to manage her financial or health care matters until the probate court approved him. All of that could have been avoided if the poor wife, earlier in life when she was "alive and well" had signed a durable financial power of attorney, as well as a healthcare proxy.

Sadly, not all love stories have a happy ending.

The most common way to avoid probate is to create a **Trust** (our Treasure Chest) to hold your assets instead of a Will.

Again, when discussing probate, there are two specific areas that need to be dealt with: ***Disability Probate*** and ***Death Probate***. Let's take each separately.

There will come a time when someone can't make their own decisions on behalf of their well-being. It could be a cognitive impairment associated with aging, like Alzheimer's or dementia or a traumatic event like a stroke or heart attack. Now you're still alive, but you're "alive and not-so well." **Disability Probate** comes into focus. And let's be very clear about one thing, you ***do not*** want the courts making those life or death decisions on your behalf. To avoid this you have to create, with your elder law attorney, an updated durable power of attorney and a healthcare proxy, giving your family or your "helpers" legal authority and powers to make these decisions for you. I recall one time a court appointed attorney was appointed as a "conservator" for an elderly woman in a nursing home. This was because the woman did not have a durable power of attorney and she was in a nursing home with dementia. She had financial means to pay the nursing home but did not have the capacity to pay her bills. The nursing home petitioned the probate court to have a conservator appointed to handle her finances which would include paying the nursing home. The attorney worked on the matter for six months and the woman incurred a legal bill of $50,000. And it's also very important that you **do not** assume the power of attorney you took out several years ago is still valid. It may not have a shelf life in lieu of recent changes in Massachusetts probate law. Also, I strongly recommend anyone 65 years of age and older should have a durable power of attorney with "enhanced elder law" powers.

Death Probate is a beast of a different color. Everything owned by a person who has died is known as their estate. The estate may be made up of:

- Money, both cash and money in a bank. This could include money paid out on a life insurance policy

- Money owed to the person who has died

- Shares of stock

- Property, for example, their home

- Personal possessions, for example, their car or jewelry

- Retirement assets, 401k, IRA

- Investment Assets, Mutual Funds, Money Markets

If the person who died owes money to other people, for example, on a credit card, or a mortgage, this comes out of the estate. The estate of the person who has died is usually passed to surviving relatives and friends, either according to instructions in the Will, or if the person dies without a Will, also known as, the "government plan." Even though a Will does not provide any protections from the Four-Headed Monster, at least you can spell out who is in charge and who gets your possessions when you are gone. Not ideal, but better than the government plan where the laws of intestate will say who gets your possessions which could include unintended beneficiaries.

THE FOUR-HEADED MONSTER: *ESTATE "DEATH" TAXES*

We have all heard the old saying, "There is nothing certain except death and taxes." Well, leave it up to the Commonwealth of Massachusetts to combine "death" and "taxes" into one sandwich, the kind you do not want to take a bite of. Thus, the Estate "Death" Tax because your estate (everything you own) is taxed at your death if the value of all the assets is $1 million or more.

For Massachusetts residents, if your estate is worth $1 million or more, money must be paid to the state first before any assets are passed on following your death. Under current Massachusetts law the estate tax has a range of 0.8% to 16%. The value for the entire estate is calculated on such things as the value of your home or homes, plus life insurance, savings accounts and retirement accounts. In addition, the state taxes you starting from dollar one, not just what is above the $1 million threshold.

Here's a good example. A couple of years ago, a young man came into my elder law care center with a milk crate full of probate documents. His dad was in an assisted living facility and had a simple Will. But he also had a $1.2 million estate. When the son came in with the milk crate he understood that they were getting bitten by the probate court monster but he was not aware that the estate tax monster was also about to take a big bite out of the estate, too. We added everything up and then we tried to get the value under one million. Unfortunately, as hard as we tried, we didn't have enough deductions to achieve our goal. There was no house, there was no mortgage, or anything like that. We just had funeral expenses and some legal and accounting costs. So we ended up around $1.2 million estate, which meant the son, who was the personal representative of the estate, had to write a check for about $50,000 to the Massachusetts Department of

Revenue. Ouch!

But the state is not the only one holding out their huge monster like hand. Uncle Sam will also be looking for his 40% payday. However, under current law, your estate will not owe a federal estate tax unless your taxable estate is worth more than $11 million ($22 million combined for you and your spouse).

I guess the next logical question is this: If the estate death tax is based on your net worth when you die, then why not just give your money away while you're still alive?

The answer is quite simple; the folks at the Massachusetts Department of Revenue have already anticipated your question by putting rules in place whereas large gifts will count as part of your taxable estate, even though you no longer have the money or property in your possession. However, under current law, you are allowed to give gifts of up to $15,000 per person per year, which will lower your future estate taxes, but may not avoid the estate tax altogether.

Although avoiding the estate tax is difficult if your estate is over $1 million, there may be a way to reduce those taxes through proper planning. For instance, married couples can create Credit Shelter Trusts, where you can place up to $1 million of assets in trust for the benefit of the surviving spouse at the first spouse's death. This plan can save $100,000 or more in Massachusetts estate tax at death. If you have a large life insurance policy that you intend to keep in place until your death, transferring that policy to a properly drafted and administered *Irrevocable Life Insurance Trust* (ILIT) can prevent the death benefit from being subject to estate tax at your death.

There is no way to get completely out of the path when the Massachusetts Estate Death Tax monster comes roaring down the tracks. But with proper planning, there are permissible legal strategies that can be taken to ensure you and your loved ones do not get hit head-on.

THE FOUR-HEADED MONSTER:
FINANCIAL CREDITORS & PREDATORS

Remember the story of Betty the Barmaid back in Chapter Five? How could that ugly situation have been avoided?

The goal here is to keep family money in the family, which is what we refer to as Family Bloodline Protection Trust (FBPT). And this has to be created with lock-down language so it is set in stone and resistant to any changes. These Trusts are typically multi-generational Trusts because there is always a real possibility that the client will remarry after his/her spouse dies. In such a case, the client may also find it difficult to raise the topic of a premarital agreement to protect his own assets. A properly prepared Trust for the benefit of a surviving spouse can protect the assets in the event that the surviving spouse predeceases or divorces his or her next spouse, as in the case of our friend, Joe.

A Bloodline Trust is designed to keep family money in the family, protecting the inheritance of your children and their descendants. Bloodline Trusts offer a number of important benefits:

- Trust assets can be used only for blood descendants – your children and grandchildren. Specifically, assets in the Trust can be used only for your children's or grandchildren's health, education, maintenance, or support.

- Trust assets are never available to a son- or daughter-in-law, either during the marriage or in a divorce through equitable distribution or alimony.

- Trust assets are protected from your children's creditors and those of your sons- or daughters-in-law or outlaws.

- Your child may be given control over the Trust.

- Your child, acting as trustee, can distribute principal to or for the benefit of himself/herself or to his or her descendants.

- The trust terminates at your child's death, and the remaining principal can be paid only to your child's descendants (your grandchildren) in trust.

Your child can serve as the initial trustee of the Bloodline Trust or he/she can share this responsibility with an independent co-trustee. At any time, your child can resign from the role of trustee. He or she will be removed from the role automatically in the event of a divorce or lawsuit and will be reinstated only when the divorce is complete, the divorce action is terminated, or the lawsuit is resolved. An independent successor trustee can be appointed by you in your Will or Trust, or can be nominated by your child. That successor trustee may be a financial institution or another child in the family.

Using a Family Bloodline Protection Trust allows your beneficiary children protection of their inheritance from outside threats such as; lawsuits, divorces, automobile accidents, or times of turmoil. From my experience, Wills and most Trusts give an "outright" distribution to your children or beneficiaries, putting 100% of the inheritance at risk. The Family Bloodline Protection Trust (FBPT) that we create for our clients give them better than a gift, it gives them a "protected" gift.

Sad to say, with the divorce rate around 50%, it's very possible, should you remarry, that after you're gone your hard-earned dollars could be taken from the ones you love and targeted by your new wife to her children, money that your children may have otherwise used for your grandchild's college education. And it's now in the hands of pretty much strangers.

Thankfully, by implementing a Family Bloodline Protection Trust sooner rather than later, this type of situation can be avoided. Having these protections is a nice

sweater in the suitcase to have in the event it is needed.

THE FOUR-HEADED MONSTER: *NURSING HOME*

We all have a pretty good idea where our final resting place will be when we—as Shakespeare so eloquently put it—"shuffle off this mortal coil." However, for many of us it's very likely that the second to last stop will be a nursing home. Statistical data shows us that 70% of people 70 years of age and older will need some level of long-term care assistance someday, whether it's in an assisted living facility or a nursing home. The question you need to ask yourself is, if either I or my spouse became completely incapacitated how would we pay for that $15,000 *per month* nursing home?

Now, a nursing home can be a warm, loving place, where you can make new friends and peacefully live out your days in comfort. But a nursing home also has the potential to be a giant monster taking a huge monstrous bite out of your life time savings and the beloved family home. This isn't hard to do when you are looking at a $15,000 per month bill, with an average nursing home stay of three years. Do the math… that's $540,000, over half a million dollars. Who among us can truthfully say they have that kind of money? Not many. But you might have a house worth that much… which you'll have to use to keep the financial faucet turned on at the nursing home.

I think back to my own situation. My dad ended up in nursing home. Medicare, fortunately, covered him for a period of time before they shut the faucet off. Sadly, he did not protect the family home and he regretted it terribly. And I never want my clients to have to be in that situation.

This is a very important point, and one well worth repeating. Back in Chapter One we discussed our client "Kathy." So for this story our client will be "Cindy."

Cindy wants to create an Irrevocable Medicaid Asset Protection Trust (MAPT) because she has a lot of equity in her house. So we're going to record the deed at the local registry of deeds which triggers the five-year clock to begin to run on the MAPT to beat the required "five year look-back" period under current law. But remember, as the clock begins to run, you have to stay healthy. That means not becoming disabled and not filing the Medicaid application, and so on.

Flash forward five years later and we hear that Cindy is disabled and she needs to go into a nursing home. Is the house protected?

Since Cindy stayed healthy for five years *and a day*, she legally beat the five year look back period for MassHealth Medicaid planning. Her home is off the table and theoretically protected.

What this means is if Medicaid inquires, have you transferred any assets within the past five years you can answer the question truthfully and you can say, "No, we have not transferred any assets within the past five years." Now we can proceed with the MassHealth Medicaid application and provided Cindy's other assets are either below the Medicaid threshold for eligibility or properly protected with other legal strategies, she can be approved for Medicaid benefits. Then Medicaid will pay for the $15,000 per month nursing home and that asset, her house where she raised a loving family and is full of treasured memories, the house that Cindy transferred into her MAPT a little over five years ago, is now protected for her family and for her loved ones. The key is Cindy took action when she was alive and well. She did the 3 P's, which means she *Protected* the home, *Preserved* the home and *Passed* the home down to her children as a family legacy.

You don't ever want to get in a situation where there is even a *hint* that your loved one might get evicted from a nursing home because he or she is unable to pay their bills. Nursing home evictions are an issue for many elderly people. Reports of evictions and complaints against nursing homes attempting to evict patients are widespread. Nursing homes are businesses and eviction problems often occur for residents when financial issues arise. There are federal regulations in place concerning nursing home evictions. However, it is largely dependent on the state to enforce those regulations. Some residents or their families choose to fight back with complaints and legal action. Unfortunately, many of these cases go unreported as is the case with other types of elder abuse.

Nursing homes do have guidelines that allow for evictions in certain cases. A resident may be evicted, but the facility must follow the minimum guidelines of federal and state law to be successful. One reason an elderly person may be evicted is if their clinical or behavioral status puts others in the facility in danger. This is one of the reasons often cited for discharging patients involuntarily.

Sadly though, forced discharges are also commonly attributed to the patient's care not being paid. This can happen when private pay patients run out of financial resources. Another common trigger for eviction notices occurs when Medicare patients change from being a patient under the Medicare program to requalifying under Medicaid. This transition can mean a reduction in the resources the facility is being paid. Involuntary discharge can also occur if the facility is unable to meet the resident's needs or if it is necessary for the resident's welfare. A patient's needs and the facility's ability to meet those needs should be assessed before the person is admitted to the facility. For this reason, the inability to meet a patient's needs should be a rare reason for discharge. If it is determined that the person no longer needs the care the nursing home provides, they can be discharged. Finally, if the facility is closing, patients can be legally discharged.

It is important for residents and their families to do their homework and be informed about the regulations governing nursing homes. Not only must nursing homes follow these regulations, but they must also follow strict procedural guidelines in order to evict patients. If these guidelines are not strictly followed, the discharge can be reversed. If a resident is threatened with eviction, this must be done in writing and must include a written reason for the eviction. If you or your family receives a discharge notice, contact an elder law attorney immediately. I have had the experience of advocating for my clients while we were trying to get them approved for Medicaid benefits. The Medicaid application process can be lengthy taking up to six months or longer. The nursing home can have their attorneys become aggressive with threats of legal action.

Even if the resident does not want to stay in that particular facility, it is important to take the discharge notice to an attorney because it may affect the patient's ability to get into another facility. The window for appeals is short, so be sure to contact an attorney quickly in order to give the attorney time to build the case and file the appropriate documents. The Nursing Home Reform Act helps to protect residents. The problem is that many people are not informed and miss their opportunity to appeal these evictions. Timely response is essential in these cases.

Living in a nursing home is a difficult experience for many patients and their families. A threat of eviction adds stress to an already stressful situation, especially if that stress is due to the inability to pay. The elder law attorney is your best advocate as he or she is able to enforce the resident's rights and protect them within mandatory time frames.

When is the best time to fix a leaking roof? The answer is on a sunny day. You do not want to be up on a roof fixing a leak during a thunderstorm.

Take action now and work with a qualified elder law attorney because when you don't, who stands to benefit?

RESOURCES

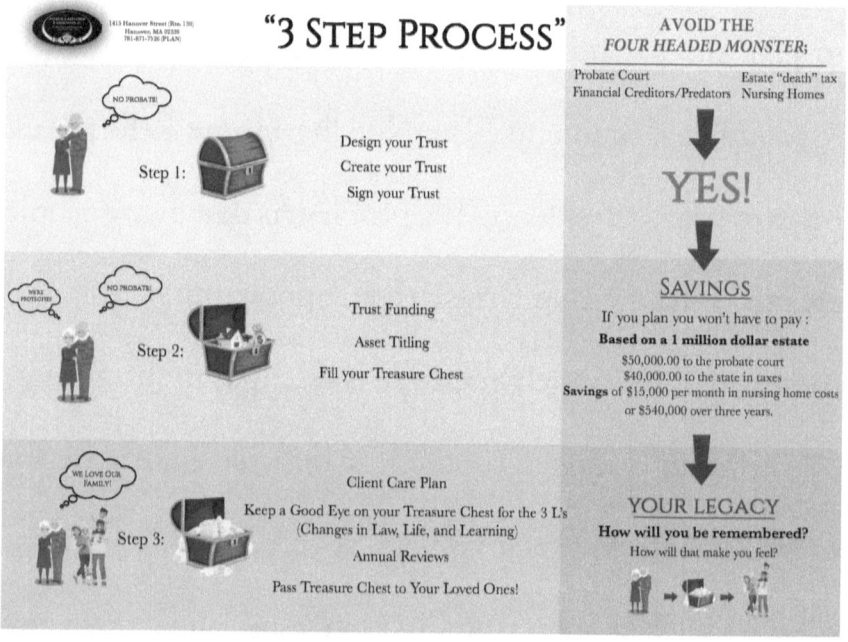

"3 STEP PROCESS"

Step 1:
Design your Trust
Create your Trust
Sign your Trust

Step 2:
Trust Funding
Asset Titling
Fill your Treasure Chest

Step 3:
Client Care Plan
Keep a Good Eye on your Treasure Chest for the 3 L's
(Changes in Law, Life, and Learning)
Annual Reviews
Pass Treasure Chest to Your Loved Ones!

AVOID THE
FOUR HEADED MONSTER;

Probate Court — Estate "death" tax
Financial Creditors/Predators — Nursing Homes

YES!

SAVINGS

If you plan you won't have to pay :
Based on a 1 million dollar estate
$50,000.00 to the probate court
$40,000.00 to the state in taxes
Savings of $15,000 per month in nursing home costs
or $540,000 over three years.

YOUR LEGACY

How will you be remembered?
How will that make you feel?

Voucher

This voucher is our gift to you for the completion of reading *How to Avoid the Four Headed Monster*! Use this voucher for a free one on one meeting with one of our attorneys [a $500 value] at a later date.

NON-TRANSFERABLE

| **ADDRESS:** 1415 Hanover Street - [Second Floor], Hanover, MA 02339 | **PHONE:** [781] 871-7526 |

| **EMAIL:** Pat@elderlawcare.com | **WEBSITE:** www.elderlawcare.com | **FAX :** [781] 871-7525 |

SAVE $500

PATRICK J. KELLEHER & ASSOCIATES, P.C.
ATTORNEYS AND COUNSELLORS AT LAW

MASSACHUSETTS RESIDENTS ONLY

ATTORNEYS & COUNSELLORS AT LAW

*Patrick J. Kelleher & Associates, P.C.

Our Three Step Process™

WeMustProtectThisHouse.com

STEP ONE

1.1 – FAMILY DESTINY MEETING

1.2 - FAMILY VISION / DESIGN MEETING

1.3 – FAMILY CELEBRATION MEETING

STEP TWO

2.1 - FAMILY TREASURE CHEST
FUNDING MEETING

2.2 – FAMILY CARE MEETING

STEP THREE

UPDATE PROCESS - Client Care Program™

FAMILY TREASURE CHEST REUNION

1.1 – FAMILY DESTINY MEETING
- Gather clients' personal and financial information
- Identify clients' family needs and planning options that take care of their family
- Educate clients about our Three Step Process

1.2 – FAMILY VISION / DESIGN MEETING
- Confirm clients' personal and financial information
- Provide counsel on available estate planning options
- Design clients' customized estate plan

1.3 – FAMILY CELEBRATION / SIGNING MEETING
- Review and sign customized estate plan
- Educate about funding process
- Discuss documents needed for funding meeting

2.1 – FAMILY TREASURE CHEST FUNDING MEETING
- Execute initial funding documents to fund assets into trust
- Review and establish funding process timeline
- Participate in follow-up meetings to continuously fund assets into trust
- Identify possible financial and tax concerns/ needs and refer to advisors

2.2 – FAMILY CARE MEETING
- Trusted family members and advisors attend meeting
- Estate plan explained, questions addressed, and potential issues discussed

Our Client Care Program™ - FAMILY TREASURE CHEST REUNION MEETING
- Yearly review and continuous update of assets
- Assistance in funding of new assets
- The 3 L's. Estate plan updated as law changes necessitate (word processing, amendments/client-initiated changes on an as-needed basis)

1415 Hanover Street, Hanover, MA 02339 781-871-PLAN (7526) - *Member, National Academy of Elder Law Attorneys and Massachusetts Estate Planning Forum

IN CLASS ASSIGNMENT

Real Estate Value: _____

"Cash" Assets

(401k, IRA, Investment Portfolios): _____

Fair Market Value of Personal Property *(cars, jewelry, etc):*

_____

_____

_____

_____

_____

VALUE OF GROSS ESTATE: _____

5% OF GROSS ESTATE: _____

1ˢᵗ Head of the Monster: Probate Court

- <u>WILL APPLY</u> to any asset in your name alone upon your passing, EVEN if you have a Will.

Amount Due to Tax Man _____

2ⁿᵈ Head of the Monster: Estate 'Death' Tax

- Estate value over $1,000,000.00   Y/N
  - If Yes, estimate $65,000 for estates 1-1.5 million, $150,000.00 for a 3 million dollar estate.

Amount at Risk _____

3ʳᵈ Head of the Monster: Creditors & Predators

- From Beau/Betty, in-laws becoming outlaws, etc.

Equity at Risk _____

4ᵗʰ Head of the Monster: Nursing Home Costs

- 3 year stay (average) = $540,000.00
- 70% of the population beyond age 70 will require some time of assisted living.

How Much Your Will or Government Plan Will Cost?

$_____

The Law Firm of Patrick J. Kelleher & Associates. P.C.

Cordially Invites You to Attend:

"THE FOUR HEADED MONSTER OF ESTATE PLANNING & ELDER LAW AND WHY YOU NEED TO AVOID IT"

Presented by:

PATRICK J. KELLEHER, ESQ.

This FREE educational Estate Planning & Elder Law Care workshop is designed to educate the attendees on how to protect their assets and family from the Four Headed Monster of estate planning & elder law!

We teach our free educational workshops monthly at our Hanover Learning Center and in other communities. Go to **ElderLawCare.com** for more information and upcoming workshops near you!

Topics to be covered include:

- **Revocable Asset Protection Trusts (RAPT) & Medicaid Asset Protection Trust (MAPT)** – what are they and why are people creating them?

- Why a **will** is woefully insufficient to protect your assets and family?

- What is the difference between a **<u>revocable</u>** and an **<u>irrevocable</u>** trust?

- Does a **will** protect my assets from probate court?

- Why should accounts be titled in the name of a trust?

- What is the cost of a **nursing home**?

- How to protect assets & family from probate, estate death taxes, financial creditors & predators, and nursing homes?

ADDITIONAL RESOURCES

Patrick J. Kelleher's Elder Law Care Center. Educational elder law videos and blog articles to teach you how to protect what you have for the people you love the most. **www.elderlawcare.com**

Estate Planning & Elder Law Training Academy and Courses. **www.PatrickJKelleher.com**

National Academy of Elder Law Attorneys. Educational and current news on elder law matters, law changes and elder law advocacy. **www.naela.org**

National Council on Aging **www.ncoa.org**

National Council for aging Care Resources for living your fullest life. **www.aginginplace.org**

Medicare Rights Center (MRC) **www.medicarerights.org**

National Meals on Wheels Program to locate a local Meals on Wheels program near you. **www.mealsonwheelsamerica.com**

American Association of Retired Persons (AARP) Non-profit organization that supports need of elderly people. **www.aarp.org**

Alzheimer's Association is the leading voluntary health organization in Alzheimer's care, support and research. **www.Alz.org**

CONTACT US

Patrick J. Kelleher & Associates, P.C.

TEL: 781-871-PLAN (7526)

FAX: 781-871-7525

Website: **www.ElderLawCare.com**

Email Patrick Kelleher: pat@elderlawcare.com

Main Office:
1415 Hanover Street (Rte 139), Second Floor
Hanover, MA 02339

Our Other Location *(By Appointment Only)*:
One Adams Place
859 Willard Street, Suite 400
Quincy, MA 02169

Mom and Dad Kelleher
The Love of Family!

NOTES

NOTES

NOTES

NOTES

www.ingramcontent.com/pod-product-compliance
Lightning Source LLC
Chambersburg PA
CBHW030939240526
45463CB00015B/727